# THE ATTORNEY GENERAL'S GUIDELINES FOR DOMESTIC FBI OPERATIONS

# PREAMBLE

These Guidelines are issued under the authority of the Attorney General as provided in sections 509, 510, 533, and 534 of title 28, United States Code, and Executive Order 12333. They apply to domestic investigative activities of the Federal Bureau of Investigation (FBI) and other activities as provided herein.

# TABLE OF CONTENTS

INTRODUCTION ................................................. 5
    A.   FBI RESPONSIBILITIES – FEDERAL CRIMES, THREATS TO THE
         NATIONAL SECURITY, FOREIGN INTELLIGENCE ............... 6
    B.   THE FBI AS AN INTELLIGENCE AGENCY ...................... 9
    C.  OVERSIGHT ........................................... 10

I.    GENERAL AUTHORITIES AND PRINCIPLES ................. 12
    A.   SCOPE ................................................ 12
    B.   GENERAL AUTHORITIES ................................ 12
    C.   USE OF AUTHORITIES AND METHODS ................... 12
    D.   NATURE AND APPLICATION OF THE GUIDELINES ............. 14

II.   INVESTIGATIONS AND INTELLIGENCE GATHERING ................. 16
    A.   ASSESSMENTS ......................................... 19
    B.   PREDICATED INVESTIGATIONS ......................... 20
    C.   ENTERPRISE INVESTIGATIONS ......................... 23

III.  ASSISTANCE TO OTHER AGENCIES ...................... 25
    A.   THE INTELLIGENCE COMMUNITY ..................... 25
    B.   FEDERAL AGENCIES GENERALLY ..................... 25
    C.   STATE, LOCAL, OR TRIBAL AGENCIES ................... 27
    D.   FOREIGN AGENCIES ................................ 27
    E.   APPLICABLE STANDARDS AND PROCEDURES ............. 28

IV.  INTELLIGENCE ANALYSIS AND PLANNING ................. 29
    A.   STRATEGIC INTELLIGENCE ANALYSIS ..................... 29
    B.   REPORTS AND ASSESSMENTS GENERALLY ................... 29
    C.   INTELLIGENCE SYSTEMS ................................ 29

V.   AUTHORIZED METHODS ................................ 31
    A.   PARTICULAR METHODS ................................ 31
    B.   SPECIAL REQUIREMENTS ................................ 32
    C.   OTHERWISE ILLEGAL ACTIVITY ......................... 33

VI.  RETENTION AND SHARING OF INFORMATION ...................... 35
    A.   RETENTION OF INFORMATION ......................... 35
    B.   INFORMATION SHARING GENERALLY ..................... 35
    C.   INFORMATION RELATING TO CRIMINAL MATTERS ............. 36
    D.   INFORMATION RELATING TO NATIONAL SECURITY AND
         FOREIGN INTELLIGENCE MATTERS ......................... 37

**VII.**   **DEFINITIONS** . . . . . . . . . . . . . . . . . . . . . . . . . . . . . . . . . . . . . . . . . . . . 42

# INTRODUCTION

As the primary investigative agency of the federal government, the Federal Bureau of Investigation (FBI) has the authority and responsibility to investigate all violations of federal law that are not exclusively assigned to another federal agency. The FBI is further vested by law and by Presidential directives with the primary role in carrying out investigations within the United States of threats to the national security. This includes the lead domestic role in investigating international terrorist threats to the United States, and in conducting counterintelligence activities to meet foreign entities' espionage and intelligence efforts directed against the United States. The FBI is also vested with important functions in collecting foreign intelligence as a member agency of the U.S. Intelligence Community. The FBI accordingly plays crucial roles in the enforcement of federal law and the proper administration of justice in the United States, in the protection of the national security, and in obtaining information needed by the United States for the conduct of its foreign affairs. These roles reflect the wide range of the FBI's current responsibilities and obligations, which require the FBI to be both an agency that effectively detects, investigates, and prevents crimes, and an agency that effectively protects the national security and collects intelligence.

The general objective of these Guidelines is the full utilization of all authorities and investigative methods, consistent with the Constitution and laws of the United States, to protect the United States and its people from terrorism and other threats to the national security, to protect the United States and its people from victimization by all crimes in violation of federal law, and to further the foreign intelligence objectives of the United States. At the same time, it is axiomatic that the FBI must conduct its investigations and other activities in a lawful and reasonable manner that respects liberty and privacy and avoids unnecessary intrusions into the lives of law-abiding people. The purpose of these Guidelines, therefore, is to establish consistent policy in such matters. They will enable the FBI to perform its duties with effectiveness, certainty, and confidence, and will provide the American people with a firm assurance that the FBI is acting properly under the law.

The issuance of these Guidelines represents the culmination of the historical evolution of the FBI and the policies governing its domestic operations subsequent to the September 11, 2001, terrorist attacks on the United States. Reflecting decisions and directives of the President and the Attorney General, inquiries and enactments of Congress, and the conclusions of national commissions, it was recognized that the FBI's functions needed to be expanded and better integrated to meet contemporary realities:

> [C]ontinuing coordination . . . is necessary to optimize the FBI's performance in both national security and criminal investigations . . . . [The] new reality requires first that the FBI and other agencies do a better job of gathering intelligence inside the United States, and second that we eliminate the remnants of the old "wall" between foreign intelligence and domestic law enforcement. Both tasks must be accomplished without sacrificing our domestic liberties and the rule of law, and both depend on building a very

different FBI from the one we had on September 10, 2001. (Report of the Commission on the Intelligence Capabilities of the United States Regarding Weapons of Mass Destruction 466, 452 (2005).)

In line with these objectives, the FBI has reorganized and reoriented its programs and missions, and the guidelines issued by the Attorney General for FBI operations have been extensively revised over the past several years. Nevertheless, the principal directives of the Attorney General governing the FBI's conduct of criminal investigations, national security investigations, and foreign intelligence collection have persisted as separate documents involving different standards and procedures for comparable activities. These Guidelines effect a more complete integration and harmonization of standards, thereby providing the FBI and other affected Justice Department components with clearer, more consistent, and more accessible guidance for their activities, and making available to the public in a single document the basic body of rules for the FBI's domestic operations.

These Guidelines also incorporate effective oversight measures involving many Department of Justice and FBI components, which have been adopted to ensure that all FBI activities are conducted in a manner consistent with law and policy.

The broad operational areas addressed by these Guidelines are the FBI's conduct of investigative and intelligence gathering activities, including cooperation and coordination with other components and agencies in such activities, and the intelligence analysis and planning functions of the FBI.

## A. FBI RESPONSIBILITIES – FEDERAL CRIMES, THREATS TO THE NATIONAL SECURITY, FOREIGN INTELLIGENCE

Part II of these Guidelines authorizes the FBI to carry out investigations to detect, obtain information about, or prevent or protect against federal crimes or threats to the national security or to collect foreign intelligence. The major subject areas of information gathering activities under these Guidelines – federal crimes, threats to the national security, and foreign intelligence – are not distinct, but rather overlap extensively. For example, an investigation relating to international terrorism will invariably crosscut these areas because international terrorism is included under these Guidelines' definition of "threat to the national security," because international terrorism subject to investigation within the United States usually involves criminal acts that violate federal law, and because information relating to international terrorism also falls within the definition of "foreign intelligence." Likewise, counterintelligence activities relating to espionage are likely to concern matters that constitute threats to the national security, that implicate violations or potential violations of federal espionage laws, and that involve information falling under the definition of "foreign intelligence."

While some distinctions in the requirements and procedures for investigations are necessary in different subject areas, the general design of these Guidelines is to take a uniform approach wherever possible, thereby promoting certainty and consistency regarding the applicable standards and facilitating compliance with those standards. Hence, these Guidelines do not require that the FBI's information gathering activities be differentially labeled as "criminal investigations," "national security investigations," or "foreign intelligence collections," or that the categories of FBI personnel who carry out investigations be segregated from each other based on the subject areas in which they operate. Rather, all of the FBI's legal authorities are available for deployment in all cases to which they apply to protect the public from crimes and threats to the national security and to further the United States' foreign intelligence objectives. In many cases, a single investigation will be supportable as an exercise of a number of these authorities – i.e., as an investigation of a federal crime or crimes, as an investigation of a threat to the national security, and/or as a collection of foreign intelligence.

## 1. Federal Crimes

The FBI has the authority to investigate all federal crimes that are not exclusively assigned to other agencies. In most ordinary criminal investigations, the immediate objectives include such matters as: determining whether a federal crime has occurred or is occurring, or if planning or preparation for such a crime is taking place; identifying, locating, and apprehending the perpetrators; and obtaining the evidence needed for prosecution. Hence, close cooperation and coordination with federal prosecutors in the United States Attorneys' Offices and the Justice Department litigating divisions are essential both to ensure that agents have the investigative tools and legal advice at their disposal for which prosecutorial assistance or approval is needed, and to ensure that investigations are conducted in a manner that will lead to successful prosecution. Provisions in many parts of these Guidelines establish procedures and requirements for such coordination.

## 2. Threats to the National Security

The FBI's authority to investigate threats to the national security derives from the executive order concerning U.S. intelligence activities, from delegations of functions by the Attorney General, and from various statutory sources. See, e.g., E.O. 12333; 50 U.S.C. 401 et seq.; 50 U.S.C. 1801 et seq. These Guidelines (Part VII.S) specifically define threats to the national security to mean: international terrorism; espionage and other intelligence activities, sabotage, and assassination, conducted by, for, or on behalf of foreign powers, organizations, or persons; foreign computer intrusion; and other matters determined by the Attorney General, consistent with Executive Order 12333 or any successor order.

Activities within the definition of "threat to the national security" that are subject to investigation under these Guidelines commonly involve violations (or potential violations) of federal criminal laws. Hence, investigations of such threats may constitute an exercise both of the FBI's criminal investigation authority and of the FBI's authority to investigate threats to the national security. As with criminal investigations generally, detecting and solving the crimes, and eventually arresting and prosecuting the perpetrators, are likely to be among the objectives of investigations relating to threats to the national security. But these investigations also often serve important purposes outside the ambit of normal criminal investigation and prosecution, by providing the basis for, and informing decisions concerning, other measures needed to protect the national security. These measures may include, for example: excluding or removing persons involved in terrorism or espionage from the United States; recruitment of double agents; freezing assets of organizations that engage in or support terrorism; securing targets of terrorism or espionage; providing threat information and warnings to other federal, state, local, and private agencies and entities; diplomatic or military actions; and actions by other intelligence agencies to counter international terrorism or other national security threats.

In line with this broad range of purposes, investigations of threats to the national security present special needs to coordinate with other Justice Department components, including particularly the Justice Department's National Security Division, and to share information and cooperate with other agencies with national security responsibilities, including other agencies of the U.S. Intelligence Community, the Department of Homeland Security, and relevant White House (including National Security Council and Homeland Security Council) agencies and entities. Various provisions in these Guidelines establish procedures and requirements to facilitate such coordination.

### 3. Foreign Intelligence

As with the investigation of threats to the national security, the FBI's authority to collect foreign intelligence derives from a mixture of administrative and statutory sources. See, e.g., E.O. 12333; 50 U.S.C. 401 et seq.; 50 U.S.C. 1801 et seq.; 28 U.S.C. 532 note (incorporating P.L. 108-458 §§ 2001-2003). These Guidelines (Part VII.E) define foreign intelligence to mean "information relating to the capabilities, intentions, or activities of foreign governments or elements thereof, foreign organizations or foreign persons, or international terrorists."

The FBI's foreign intelligence collection activities have been expanded by legislative and administrative reforms subsequent to the September 11, 2001, terrorist attacks, reflecting the FBI's role as the primary collector of foreign intelligence within the United States, and the recognized imperative that the United States' foreign intelligence collection activities become more flexible, more proactive, and more efficient in order to protect the homeland and adequately inform the United States' crucial decisions in its dealings with the rest of the world:

> The collection of information is the foundation of everything that the Intelligence Community does. While successful collection cannot ensure a good analytical product, the failure to collect information . . . turns analysis into guesswork. And as our review demonstrates, the Intelligence Community's human and technical intelligence collection agencies have collected far too little information on many of the issues we care about most. (Report of the Commission on the Intelligence Capabilities of the United States Regarding Weapons of Mass Destruction 351 (2005).)

8

These Guidelines accordingly provide standards and procedures for the FBI's foreign intelligence collection activities that meet current needs and realities and optimize the FBI's ability to discharge its foreign intelligence collection functions.

The authority to collect foreign intelligence extends the sphere of the FBI's information gathering activities beyond federal crimes and threats to the national security, and permits the FBI to seek information regarding a broader range of matters relating to foreign powers, organizations, or persons that may be of interest to the conduct of the United States' foreign affairs. The FBI's role is central to the effective collection of foreign intelligence within the United States because the authorized domestic activities of other intelligence agencies are more constrained than those of the FBI under applicable statutes and Executive Order 12333. In collecting foreign intelligence, the FBI will generally be guided by nationally-determined intelligence requirements, including the National Intelligence Priorities Framework and the National HUMINT Collection Directives, or any successor directives issued under the authority of the Director of National Intelligence (DNI). As provided in Part VII.F of these Guidelines, foreign intelligence requirements may also be established by the President or Intelligence Community officials designated by the President, and by the Attorney General, the Deputy Attorney General, or an official designated by the Attorney General.

The general guidance of the FBI's foreign intelligence collection activities by DNI-authorized requirements does not, however, limit the FBI's authority to conduct investigations supportable on the basis of its other authorities – to investigate federal crimes and threats to the national security – in areas in which the information sought also falls under the definition of foreign intelligence. The FBI conducts investigations of federal crimes and threats to the national security based on priorities and strategic objectives set by the Department of Justice and the FBI, independent of DNI-established foreign intelligence collection requirements.

Since the authority to collect foreign intelligence enables the FBI to obtain information pertinent to the United States' conduct of its foreign affairs, even if that information is not related to criminal activity or threats to the national security, the information so gathered may concern lawful activities. The FBI should accordingly operate openly and consensually with U.S. persons to the extent practicable when collecting foreign intelligence that does not concern criminal activities or threats to the national security.

## B.    THE FBI AS AN INTELLIGENCE AGENCY

The FBI is an intelligence agency as well as a law enforcement agency. Its basic functions accordingly extend beyond limited investigations of discrete matters, and include broader analytic and planning functions. The FBI's responsibilities in this area derive from various administrative and statutory sources. See, e.g., E.O. 12333; 28 U.S.C. 532 note (incorporating P.L. 108-458 §§ 2001-2003) and 534 note (incorporating P.L. 109-162 § 1107). Enhancement of the FBI's intelligence analysis capabilities and functions has consistently been recognized as a key priority in the legislative and administrative reform efforts following the

September 11, 2001, terrorist attacks:

> [Counterterrorism] strategy should . . . encompass specific efforts to . . . enhance the depth and quality of domestic intelligence collection and analysis . . . . [T]he FBI should strengthen and improve its domestic [intelligence] capability as fully and expeditiously as possible by immediately instituting measures to . . . significantly improve strategic analytical capabilities . . . . (Joint Inquiry into Intelligence Community Activities Before and After the Terrorist Attacks of September 11, 2001, S. Rep. No. 351 & H.R. Rep. No. 792, 107th Cong., 2d Sess. 4-7 (2002) (errata print).)

> A "smart" government would *integrate* all sources of information to see the enemy as a whole. Integrated all-source analysis should also inform and shape strategies to collect more intelligence. . . . The importance of integrated, all-source analysis cannot be overstated. Without it, it is not possible to "connect the dots." (Final Report of the National Commission on Terrorist Attacks Upon the United States 401, 408 (2004).)

Part IV of these Guidelines accordingly authorizes the FBI to engage in intelligence analysis and planning, drawing on all lawful sources of information. The functions authorized under that Part include: (i) development of overviews and analyses concerning threats to and vulnerabilities of the United States and its interests, (ii) research and analysis to produce reports and assessments concerning matters relevant to investigative activities or other authorized FBI activities, and (iii) the operation of intelligence systems that facilitate and support investigations through the compilation and analysis of data and information on an ongoing basis.

## C.    OVERSIGHT

The activities authorized by these Guidelines must be conducted in a manner consistent with all applicable laws, regulations, and policies, including those protecting privacy and civil liberties. The Justice Department's National Security Division and the FBI's Inspection Division, Office of General Counsel, and Office of Integrity and Compliance, along with other components, share the responsibility to ensure that the Department meets these goals with respect to national security and foreign intelligence matters. In particular, the National Security Division's Oversight Section, in conjunction with the FBI's Office of General Counsel, is responsible for conducting regular reviews of all aspects of FBI national security and foreign intelligence activities. These reviews, conducted at FBI field offices and headquarter units, broadly examine such activities for compliance with these Guidelines and other applicable requirements.

Various features of these Guidelines facilitate the National Security Division's oversight functions. Relevant requirements and provisions include: (i) required notification by the FBI to the National Security Division concerning full investigations that involve foreign intelligence collection or investigation of United States persons in relation to threats of the national security, (ii) annual reports by the FBI to the National Security Division concerning the FBI's foreign intelligence collection program, including information on the scope and nature of foreign intelligence collection activities in each FBI field office, and (iii) access by the National Security Division to information obtained by the FBI through national security or foreign intelligence activities and general authority for the Assistant Attorney General for National Security to obtain reports from the FBI concerning these activities.

Pursuant to these Guidelines, other Attorney General guidelines, and institutional assignments of responsibility within the Justice Department, additional Department components – including the Criminal Division, the United States Attorneys' Offices, and the Office of Privacy and Civil Liberties – are involved in the common endeavor with the FBI of ensuring that the activities of all Department components are lawful, appropriate, and ethical as well as effective. Examples include the involvement of both FBI and prosecutorial personnel in the review of undercover operations involving sensitive circumstances, notice requirements for investigations involving sensitive investigative matters (as defined in Part VII.N of these Guidelines), and notice and oversight provisions for enterprise investigations, which may involve a broad examination of groups implicated in the gravest criminal and national security threats. These requirements and procedures help to ensure that the rule of law is respected in the Department's activities and that public confidence is maintained in these activities.

# I. GENERAL AUTHORITIES AND PRINCIPLES

## A.    SCOPE

These Guidelines apply to investigative activities conducted by the FBI within the United States or outside the territories of all countries. They do not apply to investigative activities of the FBI in foreign countries, which are governed by the Attorney General's Guidelines for Extraterritorial FBI Operations.

## B.    GENERAL AUTHORITIES

1.    The FBI is authorized to conduct investigations to detect, obtain information about, and prevent and protect against federal crimes and threats to the national security and to collect foreign intelligence, as provided in Part II of these Guidelines.

2.    The FBI is authorized to provide investigative assistance to other federal agencies, state, local, or tribal agencies, and foreign agencies as provided in Part III of these Guidelines.

3.    The FBI is authorized to conduct intelligence analysis and planning as provided in Part IV of these Guidelines.

4.    The FBI is authorized to retain and share information obtained pursuant to these Guidelines as provided in Part VI of these Guidelines.

## C.    USE OF AUTHORITIES AND METHODS

### 1.    Protection of the United States and Its People

The FBI shall fully utilize the authorities provided and the methods authorized by these Guidelines to protect the United States and its people from crimes in violation of federal law and threats to the national security, and to further the foreign intelligence objectives of the United States.

### 2.    Choice of Methods

a.    The conduct of investigations and other activities authorized by these Guidelines may present choices between the use of different investigative methods that are each operationally sound and effective, but that are more or less intrusive, considering such factors as the effect on the privacy and civil liberties of individuals and potential damage to reputation. The least intrusive method feasible is to be used in such situations. It is recognized, however, that the choice of methods is a matter of judgment. The FBI shall not hesitate to use any lawful method consistent with these Guidelines, even if intrusive, where the degree of intrusiveness is warranted in light of the seriousness of a criminal or national security threat or the strength of the information indicating its existence, or in light of the importance of foreign intelligence sought to the United States' interests. This point is to be particularly observed in investigations relating to terrorism.

b.    United States persons shall be dealt with openly and consensually to the extent practicable when collecting foreign intelligence that does not concern criminal activities or threats to the national security.

## 3.    Respect for Legal Rights

All activities under these Guidelines must have a valid purpose consistent with these Guidelines, and must be carried out in conformity with the Constitution and all applicable statutes, executive orders, Department of Justice regulations and policies, and Attorney General guidelines. These Guidelines do not authorize investigating or collecting or maintaining information on United States persons solely for the purpose of monitoring activities protected by the First Amendment or the lawful exercise of other rights secured by the Constitution or laws of the United States. These Guidelines also do not authorize any conduct prohibited by the Guidance Regarding the Use of Race by Federal Law Enforcement Agencies.

## 4.    Undisclosed Participation in Organizations

Undisclosed participation in organizations in activities under these Guidelines shall be conducted in accordance with FBI policy approved by the Attorney General.

## 5.    Maintenance of Records under the Privacy Act

The Privacy Act restricts the maintenance of records relating to certain activities of individuals who are United States persons, with exceptions for circumstances in which the collection of such information is pertinent to and within the scope of an authorized law enforcement activity or is otherwise authorized by statute. 5 U.S.C. 552a(e)(7). Activities authorized by these Guidelines are authorized law enforcement activities or activities for which there is otherwise statutory authority for purposes of the Privacy Act. These Guidelines, however, do not provide an exhaustive enumeration of authorized FBI law enforcement activities or FBI activities for which there is otherwise statutory authority, and no restriction is implied with respect to such activities carried out by the FBI pursuant to other authorities. Further questions about the application of the Privacy Act to authorized activities of the FBI should be addressed to the FBI Office of the General Counsel, the FBI Privacy and Civil Liberties Unit, or the Department of Justice Office of Privacy and Civil Liberties.

## D. NATURE AND APPLICATION OF THE GUIDELINES

### 1. Repealers

These Guidelines supersede the following guidelines, which are hereby repealed:

a. The Attorney General's Guidelines on General Crimes, Racketeering Enterprise and Terrorism Enterprise Investigations (May 30, 2002) and all predecessor guidelines thereto.

b. The Attorney General's Guidelines for FBI National Security Investigations and Foreign Intelligence Collection (October 31, 2003) and all predecessor guidelines thereto.

c. The Attorney General's Supplemental Guidelines for Collection, Retention, and Dissemination of Foreign Intelligence (November 29, 2006).

d. The Attorney General Procedure for Reporting and Use of Information Concerning Violations of Law and Authorization for Participation in Otherwise Illegal Activity in FBI Foreign Intelligence, Counterintelligence or International Terrorism Intelligence Investigations (August 8, 1988).

e. The Attorney General's Guidelines for Reporting on Civil Disorders and Demonstrations Involving a Federal Interest (April 5, 1976).

### 2. Status as Internal Guidance

These Guidelines are set forth solely for the purpose of internal Department of Justice guidance. They are not intended to, do not, and may not be relied upon to create any rights, substantive or procedural, enforceable by law by any party in any matter, civil or criminal, nor do they place any limitation on otherwise lawful investigative and litigative prerogatives of the Department of Justice.

### 3. Departures from the Guidelines

Departures from these Guidelines must be approved by the Director of the FBI, by the Deputy Director of the FBI, or by an Executive Assistant Director designated by the Director. If a departure is necessary without such prior approval because of the immediacy or gravity of a threat to the safety of persons or property or to the national security, the Director, the Deputy Director, or a designated Executive Assistant Director shall be notified as soon thereafter as practicable. The FBI shall provide timely written notice of departures from these Guidelines to the Criminal Division and the National Security Division, and those divisions shall notify the Attorney General and the Deputy Attorney General. Notwithstanding this paragraph, all activities in all circumstances must be carried out in a manner consistent with the Constitution and laws of the United States.

## 4. Other Activities Not Limited

These Guidelines apply to FBI activities as provided herein and do not limit other authorized activities of the FBI, such as the FBI's responsibilities to conduct background checks and inquiries concerning applicants and employees under federal personnel security programs, the FBI's maintenance and operation of national criminal records systems and preparation of national crime statistics, and the forensic assistance and administration functions of the FBI Laboratory.

## II.    INVESTIGATIONS AND INTELLIGENCE GATHERING

This Part of the Guidelines authorizes the FBI to conduct investigations to detect, obtain information about, and prevent and protect against federal crimes and threats to the national security and to collect foreign intelligence.

When an authorized purpose exists, the focus of activities authorized by this Part may be whatever the circumstances warrant. The subject of such an activity may be, for example, a particular crime or threatened crime; conduct constituting a threat to the national security; an individual, group, or organization that may be involved in criminal or national security-threatening conduct; or a topical matter of foreign intelligence interest.

Investigations may also be undertaken for protective purposes in relation to individuals, groups, or other entities that may be targeted for criminal victimization or acquisition, or for terrorist attack or other depredations by the enemies of the United States. For example, the participation of the FBI in special events management, in relation to public events or other activities whose character may make them attractive targets for terrorist attack, is an authorized exercise of the authorities conveyed by these Guidelines. Likewise, FBI counterintelligence activities directed to identifying and securing facilities, personnel, or information that may be targeted for infiltration, recruitment, or acquisition by foreign intelligence services are authorized exercises of the authorities conveyed by these Guidelines.

The identification and recruitment of human sources – who may be able to provide or obtain information relating to criminal activities, information relating to terrorism, espionage, or other threats to the national security, or information relating to matters of foreign intelligence interest – is also critical to the effectiveness of the FBI's law enforcement, national security, and intelligence programs, and activities undertaken for this purpose are authorized and encouraged.

The scope of authorized activities under this Part is not limited to "investigation" in a narrow sense, such as solving particular cases or obtaining evidence for use in particular criminal prosecutions. Rather, these activities also provide critical information needed for broader analytic and intelligence purposes to facilitate the solution and prevention of crime, protect the national security, and further foreign intelligence objectives. These purposes include use of the information in intelligence analysis and planning under Part IV, and dissemination of the information to other law enforcement, Intelligence Community, and White House agencies under Part VI. Information obtained at all stages of investigative activity is accordingly to be retained and disseminated for these purposes as provided in these Guidelines, or in FBI policy consistent with these Guidelines, regardless of whether it furthers investigative objectives in a narrower or more immediate sense.

In the course of activities under these Guidelines, the FBI may incidentally obtain information relating to matters outside of its areas of primary investigative responsibility. For example, information relating to violations of state or local law or foreign law may be incidentally obtained in the course of investigating federal crimes or threats to the national security or in collecting foreign intelligence. These Guidelines do not bar the acquisition of such information in the course of authorized investigative activities, the retention of such information, or its dissemination as appropriate to the responsible authorities in other agencies or jurisdictions. Part VI of these Guidelines includes specific authorizations and requirements for sharing such information with relevant agencies and officials.

This Part authorizes different levels of information gathering activity, which afford the FBI flexibility, under appropriate standards and procedures, to adapt the methods utilized and the information sought to the nature of the matter under investigation and the character of the information supporting the need for investigation.

Assessments, authorized by Subpart A of this Part, require an authorized purpose but not any particular factual predication. For example, to carry out its central mission of preventing the commission of terrorist acts against the United States and its people, the FBI must proactively draw on available sources of information to identify terrorist threats and activities. It cannot be content to wait for leads to come in through the actions of others, but rather must be vigilant in detecting terrorist activities to the full extent permitted by law, with an eye towards early intervention and prevention of acts of terrorism before they occur. Likewise, in the exercise of its protective functions, the FBI is not constrained to wait until information is received indicating that a particular event, activity, or facility has drawn the attention of those who would threaten the national security. Rather, the FBI must take the initiative to secure and protect activities and entities whose character may make them attractive targets for terrorism or espionage. The proactive investigative authority conveyed in assessments is designed for, and may be utilized by, the FBI in the discharge of these responsibilities. For example, assessments may be conducted as part of the FBI's special events management activities.

More broadly, detecting and interrupting criminal activities at their early stages, and preventing crimes from occurring in the first place, is preferable to allowing criminal plots and activities to come to fruition. Hence, assessments may be undertaken proactively with such objectives as detecting criminal activities; obtaining information on individuals, groups, or organizations of possible investigative interest, either because they may be involved in criminal or national security-threatening activities or because they may be targeted for attack or victimization by such activities; and identifying and assessing individuals who may have value as human sources. For example, assessment activities may involve proactively surfing the Internet to find publicly accessible websites and services through which recruitment by terrorist organizations and promotion of terrorist crimes is openly taking place; through which child pornography is advertised and traded; through which efforts are made by sexual predators to lure children for purposes of sexual abuse; or through which fraudulent schemes are perpetrated against the public.

The methods authorized in assessments are generally those of relatively low intrusiveness, such as obtaining publicly available information, checking government records, and requesting information from members of the public. These Guidelines do not impose supervisory approval requirements in assessments, given the types of techniques that are authorized at this stage (e.g., perusing the Internet for publicly available information). However, FBI policy will prescribe supervisory approval requirements for certain assessments, considering such matters as the purpose of the assessment and the methods being utilized.

Beyond the proactive information gathering functions described above, assessments may be used when allegations or other information concerning crimes or threats to the national security is received or obtained, and the matter can be checked out or resolved through the relatively non-intrusive methods authorized in assessments. The checking of investigative leads in this manner can avoid the need to proceed to more formal levels of investigative activity, if the results of an assessment indicate that further investigation is not warranted.

Subpart B of this Part authorizes a second level of investigative activity, predicated investigations. The purposes or objectives of predicated investigations are essentially the same as those of assessments, but predication as provided in these Guidelines is needed – generally, allegations, reports, facts or circumstances indicative of possible criminal or national security-threatening activity, or the potential for acquiring information responsive to foreign intelligence requirements – and supervisory approval must be obtained, to initiate predicated investigations. Corresponding to the stronger predication and approval requirements, all lawful methods may be used in predicated investigations. A classified directive provides further specification concerning circumstances supporting certain predicated investigations.

Predicated investigations that concern federal crimes or threats to the national security are subdivided into preliminary investigations and full investigations. Preliminary investigations may be initiated on the basis of any allegation or information indicative of possible criminal or national security-threatening activity, but more substantial factual predication is required for full investigations. While time limits are set for the completion of preliminary investigations, full investigations may be pursued without preset limits on their duration.

The final investigative category under this Part of the Guidelines is enterprise investigations, authorized by Subpart C, which permit a general examination of the structure, scope, and nature of certain groups and organizations. Enterprise investigations are a type of full investigations. Hence, they are subject to the purpose, approval, and predication requirements that apply to full investigations, and all lawful methods may be used in carrying them out. The distinctive characteristic of enterprise investigations is that they concern groups or organizations that may be involved in the most serious criminal or national security threats to the public – generally, patterns of racketeering activity, terrorism or other threats to the national security, or the commission of offenses characteristically involved in terrorism as described in 18 U.S.C. 2332b(g)(5)(B). A broad examination of the characteristics of groups satisfying these criteria is authorized in enterprise investigations, including any relationship of the group to a foreign power, its size and composition, its geographic dimensions and finances, its past acts and goals, and its capacity for harm.

## A. ASSESSMENTS

### 1. Purposes

Assessments may be carried out to detect, obtain information about, or prevent or protect against federal crimes or threats to the national security or to collect foreign intelligence.

### 2. Approval

The conduct of assessments is subject to any supervisory approval requirements prescribed by FBI policy.

### 3. Authorized Activities

Activities that may be carried out for the purposes described in paragraph 1. in an assessment include:

a. seeking information, proactively or in response to investigative leads, relating to:

    i. activities constituting violations of federal criminal law or threats to the national security,

    ii. the involvement or role of individuals, groups, or organizations in such activities; or

    iii. matters of foreign intelligence interest responsive to foreign intelligence requirements;

b. identifying and obtaining information about potential targets of or vulnerabilities to criminal activities in violation of federal law or threats to the national security;

c. seeking information to identify potential human sources, assess the suitability, credibility, or value of individuals as human sources, validate human sources, or maintain the cover or credibility of human sources, who may be able to provide or obtain information relating to criminal activities in violation of federal law, threats to the national security, or matters of foreign intelligence interest; and

d. obtaining information to inform or facilitate intelligence analysis and planning as described in Part IV of these Guidelines.

4. **Authorized Methods**

Only the following methods may be used in assessments:

a. Obtain publicly available information.

b. Access and examine FBI and other Department of Justice records, and obtain information from any FBI or other Department of Justice personnel.

c. Access and examine records maintained by, and request information from, other federal, state, local, or tribal, or foreign governmental entities or agencies.

d. Use online services and resources (whether nonprofit or commercial).

e. Use and recruit human sources in conformity with the Attorney General's Guidelines Regarding the Use of FBI Confidential Human Sources.

f. Interview or request information from members of the public and private entities.

g. Accept information voluntarily provided by governmental or private entities.

h. Engage in observation or surveillance not requiring a court order.

i. Grand jury subpoenas for telephone or electronic mail subscriber information.

## B. PREDICATED INVESTIGATIONS

### 1. Purposes

Predicated investigations may be carried out to detect, obtain information about, or prevent or protect against federal crimes or threats to the national security or to collect foreign intelligence.

### 2. Approval

The initiation of a predicated investigation requires supervisory approval at a level or levels specified by FBI policy. A predicated investigation based on paragraph 3.c. (relating to foreign intelligence) must be approved by a Special Agent in Charge or by an FBI Headquarters official as provided in such policy.

3.	**Circumstances Warranting Investigation**

A predicated investigation may be initiated on the basis of any of the following circumstances:

a.	An activity constituting a federal crime or a threat to the national security has or may have occurred, is or may be occurring, or will or may occur and the investigation may obtain information relating to the activity or the involvement or role of an individual, group, or organization in such activity.

b.	An individual, group, organization, entity, information, property, or activity is or may be a target of attack, victimization, acquisition, infiltration, or recruitment in connection with criminal activity in violation of federal law or a threat to the national security and the investigation may obtain information that would help to protect against such activity or threat.

c.	The investigation may obtain foreign intelligence that is responsive to a foreign intelligence requirement.

4.	**Preliminary and Full Investigations**

A predicated investigation relating to a federal crime or threat to the national security may be conducted as a preliminary investigation or a full investigation. A predicated investigation that is based solely on the authority to collect foreign intelligence may be conducted only as a full investigation.

a.	**Preliminary investigations**

i.	**Predication Required for Preliminary Investigations**

A preliminary investigation may be initiated on the basis of information or an allegation indicating the existence of a circumstance described in paragraph 3.a.-.b.

ii.	**Duration of Preliminary Investigations**

A preliminary investigation must be concluded within six months of its initiation, which may be extended by up to six months by the Special Agent in Charge. Extensions of preliminary investigations beyond a year must be approved by FBI Headquarters.

### iii. Methods Allowed in Preliminary Investigations

All lawful methods may be used in a preliminary investigation except for methods within the scope of Part V.A.11.-.13. of these Guidelines.

## b. Full Investigations

### i. Predication Required for Full Investigations

A full investigation may be initiated if there is an articulable factual basis for the investigation that reasonably indicates that a circumstance described in paragraph 3.a.-.b. exists or if a circumstance described in paragraph 3.c. exists.

### ii. Methods Allowed in Full Investigations

All lawful methods may be used in a full investigation.

## 5. Notice Requirements

a.  An FBI field office shall notify FBI Headquarters and the United States Attorney or other appropriate Department of Justice official of the initiation by the field office of a predicated investigation involving a sensitive investigative matter. If the investigation is initiated by FBI Headquarters, FBI Headquarters shall notify the United States Attorney or other appropriate Department of Justice official of the initiation of such an investigation. If the investigation concerns a threat to the national security, an official of the National Security Division must be notified. The notice shall identify all sensitive investigative matters involved in the investigation.

b.  The FBI shall notify the National Security Division of:

   i.   the initiation of any full investigation of a United States person relating to a threat to the national security; and

   ii.  the initiation of any full investigation that is based on paragraph 3.c. (relating to foreign intelligence).

c.  The notifications under subparagraphs a. and b. shall be made as soon as practicable, but no later than 30 days after the initiation of an investigation.

22

d.    The FBI shall notify the Deputy Attorney General if FBI Headquarters disapproves a field office's initiation of a predicated investigation relating to a threat to the national security on the ground that the predication for the investigation is insufficient.

## C.    ENTERPRISE INVESTIGATIONS

### 1.    Definition

A full investigation of a group or organization may be initiated as an enterprise investigation if there is an articulable factual basis for the investigation that reasonably indicates that the group or organization may have engaged or may be engaged in, or may have or may be engaged in planning or preparation or provision of support for:

a.    a pattern of racketeering activity as defined in 18 U.S.C. 1961(5);

b.    international terrorism or other threat to the national security;

c.    domestic terrorism as defined in 18 U.S.C. 2331(5) involving a violation of federal criminal law;

d.    furthering political or social goals wholly or in part through activities that involve force or violence and a violation of federal criminal law; or

e.    an offense described in 18 U.S.C. 2332b(g)(5)(B) or 18 U.S.C. 43.

### 2.    Scope

The information sought in an enterprise investigation may include a general examination of the structure, scope, and nature of the group or organization including: its relationship, if any, to a foreign power; the identity and relationship of its members, employees, or other persons who may be acting in furtherance of its objectives; its finances and resources; its geographical dimensions; and its past and future activities and goals.

### 3.    Notice and Reporting Requirements

a.    The responsible Department of Justice component for the purpose of notification and reports in enterprise investigations is the National Security Division, except that, for the purpose of notifications and reports in an enterprise investigation relating to a pattern of racketeering activity that does not involve an offense or offenses described in 18 U.S.C. 2332b(g)(5)(B), the responsible Department of Justice component is the

Organized Crime and Racketeering Section of the Criminal Division.

b.      An FBI field office shall notify FBI Headquarters of the initiation by the field office of an enterprise investigation.

c.      The FBI shall notify the National Security Division or the Organized Crime and Racketeering Section of the initiation of an enterprise investigation, whether by a field office or by FBI Headquarters, and the component so notified shall notify the Attorney General and the Deputy Attorney General. The FBI shall also notify any relevant United States Attorney's Office, except that any investigation within the scope of Part VI.D.1.d of these Guidelines (relating to counterintelligence investigations) is to be treated as provided in that provision. Notifications by the FBI under this subparagraph shall be provided as soon as practicable, but no later than 30 days after the initiation of the investigation.

d.      The Assistant Attorney General for National Security or the Chief of the Organized Crime and Racketeering Section, as appropriate, may at any time request the FBI to provide a report on the status of an enterprise investigation and the FBI will provide such reports as requested.

# III. ASSISTANCE TO OTHER AGENCIES

The FBI is authorized to provide investigative assistance to other federal, state, local, or tribal, or foreign agencies as provided in this Part.

The investigative assistance authorized by this Part is often concerned with the same objectives as those identified in Part II of these Guidelines – investigating federal crimes and threats to the national security, and collecting foreign intelligence. In some cases, however, investigative assistance to other agencies is legally authorized for purposes other than those identified in Part II, such as assistance in certain contexts to state or local agencies in the investigation of crimes under state or local law, see 28 U.S.C. 540, 540A, 540B, and assistance to foreign agencies in the investigation of foreign law violations pursuant to international agreements. Investigative assistance for such legally authorized purposes is permitted under this Part, even if it is not for purposes identified as grounds for investigation under Part II.

The authorities provided by this Part are cumulative to Part II and do not limit the FBI's investigative activities under Part II. For example, Subpart B.2 in this Part authorizes investigative activities by the FBI in certain circumstances to inform decisions by the President concerning the deployment of troops to deal with civil disorders, and Subpart B.3 authorizes investigative activities to facilitate demonstrations and related public health and safety measures. The requirements and limitations in these provisions for conducting investigations for the specified purposes do not limit the FBI's authority under Part II to investigate federal crimes or threats to the national security that occur in the context of or in connection with civil disorders or demonstrations.

## A. THE INTELLIGENCE COMMUNITY

The FBI may provide investigative assistance (including operational support) to authorized intelligence activities of other Intelligence Community agencies.

## B. FEDERAL AGENCIES GENERALLY

### 1. In General

The FBI may provide assistance to any federal agency in the investigation of federal crimes or threats to the national security or in the collection of foreign intelligence, and investigative assistance to any federal agency for any other purpose that may be legally authorized, including investigative assistance to the Secret Service in support of its protective responsibilities.

### 2. The President in Relation to Civil Disorders

    a.    At the direction of the Attorney General, the Deputy Attorney General, or the Assistant Attorney General for the Criminal Division, the FBI shall collect information relating to actual or threatened civil disorders to assist the President in determining (pursuant to the authority of the President under 10 U.S.C. 331-33) whether use of the armed forces or militia is required and how a decision to commit troops should be implemented. The information sought shall concern such matters as:

    i.    The size of the actual or threatened disorder, both in number of people involved or affected and in geographic area.

    ii.    The potential for violence.

    iii.    The potential for expansion of the disorder in light of community conditions and underlying causes of the disorder.

    iv.    The relationship of the actual or threatened disorder to the enforcement of federal law or court orders and the likelihood that state or local authorities will assist in enforcing those laws or orders.

    v.    The extent of state or local resources available to handle the disorder.

b.    Investigations under this paragraph will be authorized only for a period of 30 days, but the authorization may be renewed for subsequent 30 day periods.

c.    Notwithstanding Subpart E.2 of this Part, the methods that may be used in an investigation under this paragraph are those described in subparagraphs a.-.d., subparagraph f. (other than pretext interviews or requests), or subparagraph g. of Part II.A.4 of these Guidelines. The Attorney General, the Deputy Attorney General, or the Assistant Attorney General for the Criminal Division may also authorize the use of other methods described in Part II.A.4.

### 3. Public Health and Safety Authorities in Relation to Demonstrations

a.    At the direction of the Attorney General, the Deputy Attorney General, or the Assistant Attorney General for the Criminal Division, the FBI shall collect information relating to demonstration activities that are likely to require the federal government to take action to facilitate the activities and provide public health and safety measures with respect to those activities. The information sought in such an investigation shall be that needed to facilitate an adequate federal response to ensure public health and safety and to protect the exercise of First Amendment rights, such as:

    i.    The time, place, and type of activities planned.

    ii.    The number of persons expected to participate.

    iii.    The expected means and routes of travel for participants and expected time of arrival.

    iv.    Any plans for lodging or housing of participants in connection with the demonstration.

    b.    Notwithstanding Subpart E.2 of this Part, the methods that may be used in an investigation under this paragraph are those described in subparagraphs a.-.d., subparagraph f. (other than pretext interviews or requests), or subparagraph g. of Part II.A.4 of these Guidelines. The Attorney General, the Deputy Attorney General, or the Assistant Attorney General for the Criminal Division may also authorize the use of other methods described in Part II.A.4.

## C.   STATE, LOCAL, OR TRIBAL AGENCIES

The FBI may provide investigative assistance to state, local, or tribal agencies in the investigation of matters that may involve federal crimes or threats to the national security, or for such other purposes as may be legally authorized.

## D.   FOREIGN AGENCIES

1.    At the request of foreign law enforcement, intelligence, or security agencies, the FBI may conduct investigations or provide assistance to investigations by such agencies, consistent with the interests of the United States (including national security interests) and with due consideration of the effect on any United States person. Investigations or assistance under this paragraph must be approved as provided by FBI policy. The FBI shall notify the National Security Division concerning investigation or assistance under this paragraph where: (i) FBI Headquarters approval for the activity is required pursuant to the approval policy adopted by the FBI for purposes of this paragraph, and (ii) the activity relates to a threat to the national security. Notification to the National Security Division shall be made as soon as practicable but no later than 30 days after the approval. Provisions regarding notification to or coordination with the Central Intelligence Agency by the FBI in memoranda of understanding or agreements with the Central Intelligence Agency may also apply to activities under this paragraph.

2.    The FBI may not provide assistance to foreign law enforcement, intelligence, or

security officers conducting investigations within the United States unless such officers have provided prior notification to the Attorney General as required by 18 U.S.C. 951.

3.   The FBI may conduct background inquiries concerning consenting individuals when requested by foreign government agencies.

4.   The FBI may provide other material and technical assistance to foreign governments to the extent not otherwise prohibited by law.

## E.   APPLICABLE STANDARDS AND PROCEDURES

1.   Authorized investigative assistance by the FBI to other agencies under this Part includes joint operations and activities with such agencies.

2.   All lawful methods may be used in investigative assistance activities under this Part.

3.   Where the methods used in investigative assistance activities under this Part go beyond the methods authorized in assessments under Part II.A.4 of these Guidelines, the following apply:

   a.   Supervisory approval must be obtained for the activity at a level or levels specified in FBI policy.

   b.   Notice must be provided concerning sensitive investigative matters in the manner described in Part II.B.5.

   c.   A database or records system must be maintained that permits, with respect to each such activity, the prompt retrieval of the status of the activity (open or closed), the dates of opening and closing, and the basis for the activity. This database or records system may be combined with the database or records system for predicated investigations required by Part VI.A.2.

## IV. INTELLIGENCE ANALYSIS AND PLANNING

The FBI is authorized to engage in analysis and planning. The FBI's analytic activities enable the FBI to identify and understand trends, causes, and potential indicia of criminal activity and other threats to the United States that would not be apparent from the investigation of discrete matters alone. By means of intelligence analysis and strategic planning, the FBI can more effectively discover crimes, threats to the national security, and other matters of national intelligence interest and can provide the critical support needed for the effective discharge of its investigative responsibilities and other authorized activities. For example, analysis of threats in the context of special events management, concerning public events or activities that may be targeted for terrorist attack, is an authorized activity under this Part.

In carrying out its intelligence functions under this Part, the FBI is authorized to draw on all lawful sources of information, including but not limited to the results of investigative activities under these Guidelines. Investigative activities under these Guidelines and other legally authorized activities through which the FBI acquires information, data, or intelligence may properly be utilized, structured, and prioritized so as to support and effectuate the FBI's intelligence mission. The remainder of this Part provides further specification concerning activities and functions authorized as part of that mission.

### A. STRATEGIC INTELLIGENCE ANALYSIS

The FBI is authorized to develop overviews and analyses of threats to and vulnerabilities of the United States and its interests in areas related to the FBI's responsibilities, including domestic and international criminal threats and activities; domestic and international activities, circumstances, and developments affecting the national security; and matters relevant to the conduct of the United States' foreign affairs. The overviews and analyses prepared under this Subpart may encompass present, emergent, and potential threats and vulnerabilities, their contexts and causes, and identification and analysis of means of responding to them.

### B. REPORTS AND ASSESSMENTS GENERALLY

The FBI is authorized to conduct research, analyze information, and prepare reports and assessments concerning matters relevant to authorized FBI activities, such as reports and assessments concerning: types of criminals or criminal activities; organized crime groups; terrorism, espionage, or other threats to the national security; foreign intelligence matters; or the scope and nature of criminal activity in particular geographic areas or sectors of the economy.

### C. INTELLIGENCE SYSTEMS

The FBI is authorized to operate intelligence, identification, tracking, and information systems in support of authorized investigative activities, or for such other or additional purposes as may be legally authorized, such as intelligence and tracking systems relating to terrorists, gangs, or organized crime groups.

# V.    AUTHORIZED METHODS

## A.    PARTICULAR METHODS

All lawful investigative methods may be used in activities under these Guidelines as authorized by these Guidelines. Authorized methods include, but are not limited to, those identified in the following list. The methods identified in the list are in some instances subject to special restrictions or review or approval requirements as noted:

1.    The methods described in Part II.A.4 of these Guidelines.

2.    Mail covers.

3.    Physical searches of personal or real property where a warrant or court order is not legally required because there is no reasonable expectation of privacy (e.g., trash covers).

4.    Consensual monitoring of communications, including consensual computer monitoring, subject to legal review by the Chief Division Counsel or the FBI Office of the General Counsel. Where a sensitive monitoring circumstance is involved, the monitoring must be approved by the Criminal Division or, if the investigation concerns a threat to the national security or foreign intelligence, by the National Security Division.

5.    Use of closed-circuit television, direction finders, and other monitoring devices, subject to legal review by the Chief Division Counsel or the FBI Office of the General Counsel. (The methods described in this paragraph usually do not require court orders or warrants unless they involve physical trespass or non-consensual monitoring of communications, but legal review is necessary to ensure compliance with all applicable legal requirements.)

6.    Polygraph examinations.

7.    Undercover operations. In investigations relating to activities in violation of federal criminal law that do not concern threats to the national security or foreign intelligence, undercover operations must be carried out in conformity with the Attorney General's Guidelines on Federal Bureau of Investigation Undercover Operations. In investigations that are not subject to the preceding sentence because they concern threats to the national security or foreign intelligence, undercover operations involving religious or political organizations must be reviewed and approved by FBI Headquarters, with participation by the National Security Division in the review process.

8.    Compulsory process as authorized by law, including grand jury subpoenas and

other subpoenas, National Security Letters (15 U.S.C. 1681u, 1681v; 18 U.S.C. 2709; 12 U.S.C. 3414(a)(5)(A); 50 U.S.C. 436), and Foreign Intelligence Surveillance Act orders for the production of tangible things (50 U.S.C. 1861-63).

9. Accessing stored wire and electronic communications and transactional records in conformity with chapter 121 of title 18, United States Code (18 U.S.C. 2701–2712).

10. Use of pen registers and trap and trace devices in conformity with chapter 206 of title 18, United States Code (18 U.S.C. 3121-3127), or the Foreign Intelligence Surveillance Act (50 U.S.C. 1841-1846).

11. Electronic surveillance in conformity with chapter 119 of title 18, United States Code (18 U.S.C. 2510-2522), the Foreign Intelligence Surveillance Act, or Executive Order 12333 § 2.5.

12. Physical searches, including mail openings, in conformity with Rule 41 of the Federal Rules of Criminal Procedure, the Foreign Intelligence Surveillance Act, or Executive Order 12333 § 2.5. A classified directive provides additional limitation on certain searches.

13. Acquisition of foreign intelligence information in conformity with title VII of the Foreign Intelligence Surveillance Act.

## B. SPECIAL REQUIREMENTS

Beyond the limitations noted in the list above relating to particular investigative methods, the following requirements are to be observed:

### 1. Contacts with Represented Persons

Contact with represented persons may implicate legal restrictions and affect the admissibility of resulting evidence. Hence, if an individual is known to be represented by counsel in a particular matter, the FBI will follow applicable law and Department procedure concerning contact with represented individuals in the absence of prior notice to counsel. The Special Agent in Charge and the United States Attorney or their designees shall consult periodically on applicable law and Department procedure. Where issues arise concerning the consistency of contacts with represented persons with applicable attorney conduct rules, the United States Attorney's Office should consult with the Professional Responsibility Advisory Office.

2. **Use of Classified Investigative Technologies**

Inappropriate use of classified investigative technologies may risk the compromise of such technologies. Hence, in an investigation relating to activities in violation of federal criminal law that does not concern a threat to the national security or foreign intelligence, the use of such technologies must be in conformity with the Procedures for the Use of Classified Investigative Technologies in Criminal Cases.

## C.  OTHERWISE ILLEGAL ACTIVITY

1.  Otherwise illegal activity by an FBI agent or employee in an undercover operation relating to activity in violation of federal criminal law that does not concern a threat to the national security or foreign intelligence must be approved in conformity with the Attorney General's Guidelines on Federal Bureau of Investigation Undercover Operations. Approval of otherwise illegal activity in conformity with those guidelines is sufficient and satisfies any approval requirement that would otherwise apply under these Guidelines.

2.  Otherwise illegal activity by a human source must be approved in conformity with the Attorney General's Guidelines Regarding the Use of FBI Confidential Human Sources.

3.  Otherwise illegal activity by an FBI agent or employee that is not within the scope of paragraph 1. must be approved by a United States Attorney's Office or a Department of Justice Division, except that a Special Agent in Charge may authorize the following:

    a.  otherwise illegal activity that would not be a felony under federal, state, local, or tribal law;

    b.  consensual monitoring of communications, even if a crime under state, local, or tribal law;

    c.  the controlled purchase, receipt, delivery, or sale of drugs, stolen property, or other contraband;

    d.  the payment of bribes;

    e.  the making of false representations in concealment of personal identity or the true ownership of a proprietary; and

    f.  conducting a money laundering transaction or transactions involving an aggregate amount not exceeding $1 million.

33

However, in an investigation relating to a threat to the national security or foreign intelligence collection, a Special Agent in Charge may not authorize an activity that may constitute a violation of export control laws or laws that concern the proliferation of weapons of mass destruction. In such an investigation, a Special Agent in Charge may authorize an activity that may otherwise violate prohibitions of material support to terrorism only in accordance with standards established by the Director of the FBI and agreed to by the Assistant Attorney General for National Security.

4. The following activities may not be authorized:

   a. Acts of violence.

   b. Activities whose authorization is prohibited by law, including unlawful investigative methods, such as illegal electronic surveillance or illegal searches.

   Subparagraph a., however, does not limit the right of FBI agents or employees to engage in any lawful use of force, including the use of force in self-defense or defense of others or otherwise in the lawful discharge of their duties.

5. An agent or employee may engage in otherwise illegal activity that could be authorized under this Subpart without the authorization required by paragraph 3. if necessary to meet an immediate threat to the safety of persons or property or to the national security, or to prevent the compromise of an investigation or the loss of a significant investigative opportunity. In such a case, prior to engaging in the otherwise illegal activity, every effort should be made by the agent or employee to consult with the Special Agent in Charge, and by the Special Agent in Charge to consult with the United States Attorney's Office or appropriate Department of Justice Division where the authorization of that office or division would be required under paragraph 3., unless the circumstances preclude such consultation. Cases in which otherwise illegal activity occurs pursuant to this paragraph without the authorization required by paragraph 3. shall be reported as soon as possible to the Special Agent in Charge, and by the Special Agent in Charge to FBI Headquarters and to the United States Attorney's Office or appropriate Department of Justice Division.

6. In an investigation relating to a threat to the national security or foreign intelligence collection, the National Security Division is the approving component for otherwise illegal activity for which paragraph 3. requires approval beyond internal FBI approval. However, officials in other components may approve otherwise illegal activity in such investigations as authorized by the Assistant Attorney General for National Security.

## VI.    RETENTION AND SHARING OF INFORMATION

### A.    RETENTION OF INFORMATION

1.    The FBI shall retain records relating to activities under these Guidelines in accordance with a records retention plan approved by the National Archives and Records Administration.

2.    The FBI shall maintain a database or records system that permits, with respect to each predicated investigation, the prompt retrieval of the status of the investigation (open or closed), the dates of opening and closing, and the basis for the investigation.

### B.    INFORMATION SHARING GENERALLY

#### 1.    Permissive Sharing

Consistent with law and with any applicable agreements or understandings with other agencies concerning the dissemination of information they have provided, the FBI may disseminate information obtained or produced through activities under these Guidelines:

a.    within the FBI and to other components of the Department of Justice;

b.    to other federal, state, local, or tribal agencies if related to their responsibilities and, in relation to other Intelligence Community agencies, the determination whether the information is related to the recipient's responsibilities may be left to the recipient;

c.    to congressional committees as authorized by the Department of Justice Office of Legislative Affairs;

d.    to foreign agencies if the information is related to their responsibilities and the dissemination is consistent with the interests of the United States (including national security interests) and the FBI has considered the effect such dissemination may reasonably be expected to have on any identifiable United States person;

e.    if the information is publicly available, does not identify United States persons, or is disseminated with the consent of the person whom it concerns;

f.    if the dissemination is necessary to protect the safety or security of persons or property, to protect against or prevent a crime or threat to the national security, or to obtain information for the conduct of an authorized FBI investigation; or

g.  if dissemination of the information is otherwise permitted by the Privacy Act (5 U.S.C. 552a).

## 2.  Required Sharing

The FBI shall share and disseminate information as required by statutes, treaties, Executive Orders, Presidential directives, National Security Council directives, Homeland Security Council directives, and Attorney General-approved policies, memoranda of understanding, or agreements.

## C.  INFORMATION RELATING TO CRIMINAL MATTERS

### 1.  Coordination with Prosecutors

In an investigation relating to possible criminal activity in violation of federal law, the agent conducting the investigation shall maintain periodic written or oral contact with the appropriate federal prosecutor, as circumstances warrant and as requested by the prosecutor.  When, during such an investigation, a matter appears arguably to warrant prosecution, the agent shall present the relevant facts to the appropriate federal prosecutor.  Information on investigations that have been closed shall be available on request to a United States Attorney or his or her designee or an appropriate Department of Justice official.

### 2.  Criminal Matters Outside FBI Jurisdiction

When credible information is received by an FBI field office concerning serious criminal activity not within the FBI's investigative jurisdiction, the field office shall promptly transmit the information or refer the complainant to a law enforcement agency having jurisdiction, except where disclosure would jeopardize an ongoing investigation, endanger the safety of an individual, disclose the identity of a human source, interfere with a human source's cooperation, or reveal legally privileged information.  If full disclosure is not made for the reasons indicated, then, whenever feasible, the FBI field office shall make at least limited disclosure to a law enforcement agency or agencies having jurisdiction, and full disclosure shall be made as soon as the need for restricting disclosure is no longer present.  Where full disclosure is not made to the appropriate law enforcement agencies within 180 days, the FBI field office shall promptly notify FBI Headquarters in writing of the facts and circumstances concerning the criminal activity.  The FBI shall make periodic reports to the Deputy Attorney General on such nondisclosures and incomplete disclosures, in a form suitable to protect the identity of human sources.

3. **Reporting of Criminal Activity**

    a.    When it appears that an FBI agent or employee has engaged in criminal activity in the course of an investigation under these Guidelines, the FBI shall notify the United States Attorney's Office or an appropriate Department of Justice Division. When it appears that a human source has engaged in criminal activity in the course of an investigation under these Guidelines, the FBI shall proceed as provided in the Attorney General's Guidelines Regarding the Use of FBI Confidential Human Sources. When information concerning possible criminal activity by any other person appears in the course of an investigation under these Guidelines, the FBI shall initiate an investigation of the criminal activity if warranted, and shall proceed as provided in paragraph 1. or 2.

    b.    The reporting requirements under this paragraph relating to criminal activity by FBI agents or employees or human sources do not apply to otherwise illegal activity that is authorized in conformity with these Guidelines or other Attorney General guidelines or to minor traffic offenses.

## D. INFORMATION RELATING TO NATIONAL SECURITY AND FOREIGN INTELLIGENCE MATTERS

The general principle reflected in current laws and policies is that there is a responsibility to provide information as consistently and fully as possible to agencies with relevant responsibilities to protect the United States and its people from terrorism and other threats to the national security, except as limited by specific constraints on such sharing. The FBI's responsibilities in this area include carrying out the requirements of the Memorandum of Understanding Between the Intelligence Community, Federal Law Enforcement Agencies, and the Department of Homeland Security Concerning Information Sharing (March 4, 2003), or any successor memorandum of understanding or agreement. Specific requirements also exist for internal coordination and consultation with other Department of Justice components, and for provision of national security and foreign intelligence information to White House agencies, as provided in the ensuing paragraphs.

### 1. Department of Justice

    a.    The National Security Division shall have access to all information obtained by the FBI through activities relating to threats to the national security or foreign intelligence. The Director of the FBI and the Assistant Attorney General for National Security shall consult concerning these activities whenever requested by either of them, and the FBI shall provide such reports and information concerning these activities as the Assistant

Attorney General for National Security may request. In addition to any reports or information the Assistant Attorney General for National Security may specially request under this subparagraph, the FBI shall provide annual reports to the National Security Division concerning its foreign intelligence collection program, including information concerning the scope and nature of foreign intelligence collection activities in each FBI field office.

b.      The FBI shall keep the National Security Division apprised of all information obtained through activities under these Guidelines that is necessary to the ability of the United States to investigate or protect against threats to the national security, which shall include regular consultations between the FBI and the National Security Division to exchange advice and information relevant to addressing such threats through criminal prosecution or other means.

c.      Subject to subparagraphs d. and e., relevant United States Attorneys' Offices shall have access to and shall receive information from the FBI relating to threats to the national security, and may engage in consultations with the FBI relating to such threats, to the same extent as the National Security Division. The relevant United States Attorneys' Offices shall receive such access and information from the FBI field offices.

d.      In a counterintelligence investigation – i.e., an investigation relating to a matter described in Part VII.S.2 of these Guidelines – the FBI's provision of information to and consultation with a United States Attorney's Office are subject to authorization by the National Security Division. In consultation with the Executive Office for United States Attorneys and the FBI, the National Security Division shall establish policies setting forth circumstances in which the FBI will consult with the National Security Division prior to informing relevant United States Attorneys' Offices about such an investigation. The policies established by the National Security Division under this subparagraph shall (among other things) provide that:

     i.      the National Security Division will, within 30 days, authorize the FBI to share with the United States Attorneys' Offices information relating to certain espionage investigations, as defined by the policies, unless such information is withheld because of substantial national security considerations; and

     ii.      the FBI may consult freely with United States Attorneys' Offices concerning investigations within the scope of this subparagraph during an emergency, so long as the National Security Division is notified of such consultation as soon as practical after the consultation.

e.  Information shared with a United States Attorney's Office pursuant to subparagraph c. or d. shall be disclosed only to the United States Attorney or any Assistant United States Attorneys designated by the United States Attorney as points of contact to receive such information. The United States Attorneys and designated Assistant United States Attorneys shall have appropriate security clearances and shall receive training in the handling of classified information and information derived from the Foreign Intelligence Surveillance Act, including training concerning the secure handling and storage of such information and training concerning requirements and limitations relating to the use, retention, and dissemination of such information.

f.  The disclosure and sharing of information by the FBI under this paragraph is subject to any limitations required in orders issued by the Foreign Intelligence Surveillance Court, controls imposed by the originators of sensitive material, and restrictions established by the Attorney General or the Deputy Attorney General in particular cases. The disclosure and sharing of information by the FBI under this paragraph that may disclose the identity of human sources is governed by the relevant provisions of the Attorney General's Guidelines Regarding the Use of FBI Confidential Human Sources.

## 2.  White House

In order to carry out their responsibilities, the President, the Vice President, the Assistant to the President for National Security Affairs, the Assistant to the President for Homeland Security Affairs, the National Security Council and its staff, the Homeland Security Council and its staff, and other White House officials and offices require information from all federal agencies, including foreign intelligence, and information relating to international terrorism and other threats to the national security. The FBI accordingly may disseminate to the White House foreign intelligence and national security information obtained through activities under these Guidelines, subject to the following standards and procedures:

a.  Requests to the FBI for such information from the White House shall be made through the National Security Council staff or Homeland Security Council staff including, but not limited to, the National Security Council Legal and Intelligence Directorates and Office of Combating Terrorism, or through the President's Intelligence Advisory Board or the Counsel to the President.

b.   Compromising information concerning domestic officials or political organizations, or information concerning activities of United States persons intended to affect the political process in the United States, may be disseminated to the White House only with the approval of the Attorney General, based on a determination that such dissemination is needed for foreign intelligence purposes, for the purpose of protecting against international terrorism or other threats to the national security, or for the conduct of foreign affairs. However, such approval is not required for dissemination to the White House of information concerning efforts of foreign intelligence services to penetrate the White House, or concerning contacts by White House personnel with foreign intelligence service personnel.

c.   Examples of types of information that are suitable for dissemination to the White House on a routine basis include, but are not limited to:

   i.     information concerning international terrorism;

   ii.    information concerning activities of foreign intelligence services in the United States;

   iii.   information indicative of imminent hostilities involving any foreign power;

   iv.    information concerning potential cyber threats to the United States or its allies;

   v.     information indicative of policy positions adopted by foreign officials, governments, or powers, or their reactions to United States foreign policy initiatives;

   vi.    information relating to possible changes in leadership positions of foreign governments, parties, factions, or powers;

   vii.   information concerning foreign economic or foreign political matters that might have national security ramifications; and

   viii.  information set forth in regularly published national intelligence requirements.

d.   Communications by the FBI to the White House that relate to a national security matter and concern a litigation issue for a specific pending case must be made known to the Office of the Attorney General, the Office of

40

the Deputy Attorney General, or the Office of the Associate Attorney General. White House policy may specially limit or prescribe the White House personnel who may request information concerning such issues from the FBI.

e. The limitations on dissemination of information by the FBI to the White House under these Guidelines do not apply to dissemination to the White House of information acquired in the course of an FBI investigation requested by the White House into the background of a potential employee or appointee, or responses to requests from the White House under Executive Order 10450.

## 3. Special Statutory Requirements

a. Dissemination of information acquired under the Foreign Intelligence Surveillance Act is, to the extent provided in that Act, subject to minimization procedures and other requirements specified in that Act.

b. Information obtained through the use of National Security Letters under 15 U.S.C. 1681v may be disseminated in conformity with the general standards of this Part. Information obtained through the use of National Security Letters under other statutes may be disseminated in conformity with the general standards of this Part, subject to any applicable limitations in their governing statutory provisions: 12 U.S.C. 3414(a)(5)(B); 15 U.S.C. 1681u(f); 18 U.S.C. 2709(d); 50 U.S.C. 436(e).

## VII.    DEFINITIONS

A.    CONSENSUAL MONITORING: monitoring of communications for which a court order or warrant is not legally required because of the consent of a party to the communication.

B.    EMPLOYEE: an FBI employee or an employee of another agency working under the direction and control of the FBI.

C.    FOR OR ON BEHALF OF A FOREIGN POWER: the determination that activities are for or on behalf of a foreign power shall be based on consideration of the extent to which the foreign power is involved in:

1.    control or policy direction;

2.    financial or material support; or

3.    leadership, assignments, or discipline.

D.    FOREIGN COMPUTER INTRUSION: the use or attempted use of any cyber-activity or other means, by, for, or on behalf of a foreign power to scan, probe, or gain unauthorized access into one or more U.S.-based computers.

E.    FOREIGN INTELLIGENCE: information relating to the capabilities, intentions, or activities of foreign governments or elements thereof, foreign organizations or foreign persons, or international terrorists.

F.    FOREIGN INTELLIGENCE REQUIREMENTS:

1.    national intelligence requirements issued pursuant to authorization by the Director of National Intelligence, including the National Intelligence Priorities Framework and the National HUMINT Collection Directives, or any successor directives thereto;

2.    requests to collect foreign intelligence by the President or by Intelligence Community officials designated by the President; and

3.    directions to collect foreign intelligence by the Attorney General, the Deputy Attorney General, or an official designated by the Attorney General.

G.    FOREIGN POWER:

1.    a foreign government or any component thereof, whether or not recognized by the United States;

2.      a faction of a foreign nation or nations, not substantially composed of United States persons;

3.      an entity that is openly acknowledged by a foreign government or governments to be directed and controlled by such foreign government or governments;

4.      a group engaged in international terrorism or activities in preparation therefor;

5.      a foreign-based political organization, not substantially composed of United States persons; or

6.      an entity that is directed or controlled by a foreign government or governments.

H.      HUMAN SOURCE: a Confidential Human Source as defined in the Attorney General's Guidelines Regarding the Use of FBI Confidential Human Sources.

I.      INTELLIGENCE ACTIVITIES: any activity conducted for intelligence purposes or to affect political or governmental processes by, for, or on behalf of a foreign power.

J.      INTERNATIONAL TERRORISM:

Activities that:

1.      involve violent acts or acts dangerous to human life that violate federal, state, local, or tribal criminal law or would violate such law if committed within the United States or a state, local, or tribal jurisdiction;

2.      appear to be intended:

     i.      to intimidate or coerce a civilian population;

     ii.      to influence the policy of a government by intimidation or coercion; or

     iii.      to affect the conduct of a government by assassination or kidnapping; and

3.      occur totally outside the United States, or transcend national boundaries in terms of the means by which they are accomplished, the persons they appear to be intended to coerce or intimidate, or the locale in which their perpetrators operate or seek asylum.

K.      PROPRIETARY: a sole proprietorship, partnership, corporation, or other business entity operated on a commercial basis, which is owned, controlled, or operated wholly or in part on behalf of the FBI, and whose relationship with the FBI is concealed from third parties.

L. **PUBLICLY AVAILABLE:** information that has been published or broadcast for public consumption, is available on request to the public, is accessible on-line or otherwise to the public, is available to the public by subscription or purchase, could be seen or heard by any casual observer, is made available at a meeting open to the public, or is obtained by visiting any place or attending any event that is open to the public.

M. **RECORDS:** any records, databases, files, indices, information systems, or other retained information.

N. **SENSITIVE INVESTIGATIVE MATTER:** an investigative matter involving the activities of a domestic public official or political candidate (involving corruption or a threat to the national security), religious or political organization or individual prominent in such an organization, or news media, or any other matter which, in the judgment of the official authorizing an investigation, should be brought to the attention of FBI Headquarters and other Department of Justice officials.

O. **SENSITIVE MONITORING CIRCUMSTANCE:**

　1.　investigation of a member of Congress, a federal judge, a member of the Executive Branch at Executive Level IV or above, or a person who has served in such capacity within the previous two years;

　2.　investigation of the Governor, Lieutenant Governor, or Attorney General of any state or territory, or a judge or justice of the highest court of any state or territory, concerning an offense involving bribery, conflict of interest, or extortion related to the performance of official duties;

　3.　a party to the communication is in the custody of the Bureau of Prisons or the United States Marshals Service or is being or has been afforded protection in the Witness Security Program; or

　4.　the Attorney General, the Deputy Attorney General, or an Assistant Attorney General has requested that the FBI obtain prior approval for the use of consensual monitoring in a specific investigation.

P. **SPECIAL AGENT IN CHARGE:** the Special Agent in Charge of an FBI field office (including an Acting Special Agent in Charge), except that the functions authorized for Special Agents in Charge by these Guidelines may also be exercised by the Assistant Director in Charge or by any Special Agent in Charge designated by the Assistant Director in Charge in an FBI field office headed by an Assistant Director, and by FBI Headquarters officials designated by the Director of the FBI.

Q. **SPECIAL EVENTS MANAGEMENT:** planning and conduct of public events or activities whose character may make them attractive targets for terrorist attack.

R.	STATE, LOCAL, OR TRIBAL: any state or territory of the United States or political subdivision thereof, the District of Columbia, or Indian tribe.

S.	THREAT TO THE NATIONAL SECURITY:

1.	international terrorism;

2.	espionage and other intelligence activities, sabotage, and assassination, conducted by, for, or on behalf of foreign powers, organizations, or persons;

3.	foreign computer intrusion; and

4.	other matters determined by the Attorney General, consistent with Executive Order 12333 or a successor order.

T.	UNITED STATES: when used in a geographic sense, means all areas under the territorial sovereignty of the United States.

U.	UNITED STATES PERSON:

Any of the following, but not including any association or corporation that is a foreign power as defined in Subpart G.1.-.3.:

1.	an individual who is a United States citizen or an alien lawfully admitted for permanent residence;

2.	an unincorporated association substantially composed of individuals who are United States persons; or

3.	a corporation incorporated in the United States.

In applying paragraph 2., if a group or organization in the United States that is affiliated with a foreign-based international organization operates directly under the control of the international organization and has no independent program or activities in the United States, the membership of the entire international organization shall be considered in determining whether it is substantially composed of United States persons. If, however, the U.S.-based group or organization has programs or activities separate from, or in addition to, those directed by the international organization, only its membership in the United States shall be considered in determining whether it is substantially composed of United States persons. A classified directive provides further guidance concerning the determination of United States person status.